zero

0 1 2 3 4 5 6 7 8 9 10

zero one two three four five six seven eight nine ten

one ⚀

0 2 3 4 5 6 7 8 9 10

zero two three four five six seven eight nine ten

Pirates at Sea

Sally Hewitt

illustrated by Serena Feneziani

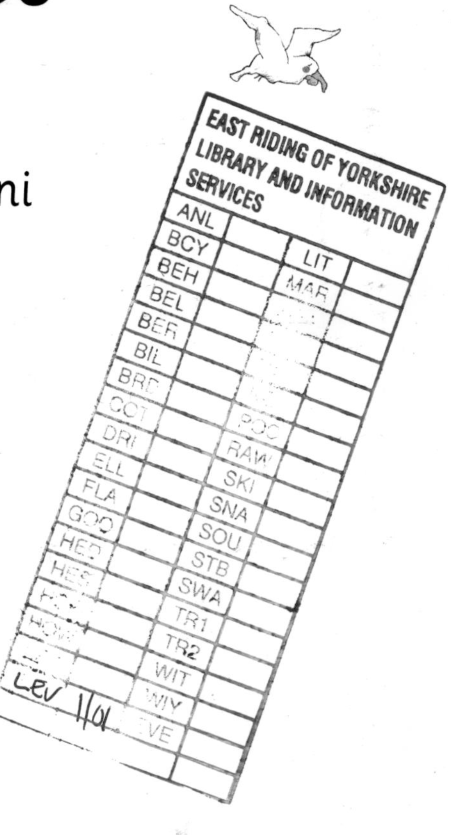

Belitha Press

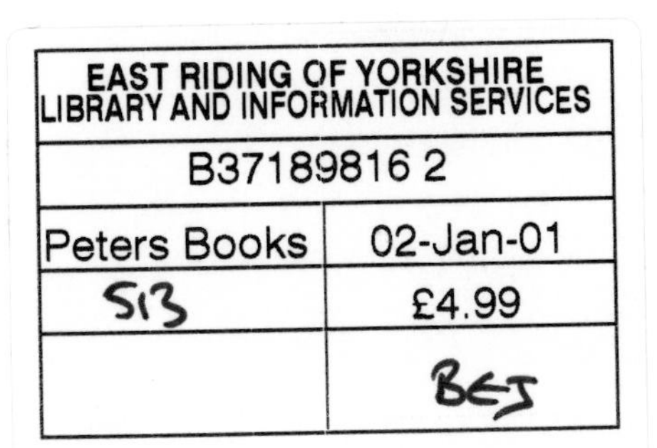

Count with the pirates

The sun rises on an empty sea.
A pirate ship sails by.
One pirate is on the lookout, but where
is the captain and the rest of the crew?
Below decks, fast asleep!

Count the pirates as they wake up one by one.
One more pirate appears on each page.
(Don't forget to count the rats, the fish
and the seagulls too!)

The first pirate has one parrot.
The second pirate has two pigtails.
What can you find to count on each pirate?

The captain puts the crew to work.
Can you help them with their tasks?

Count the tired pirates as they go to bed one by one.
There is one less pirate on each page.
The sun sets and the pirate ship sails away.
The sea is empty again.

two

2

0 1 3 4 5 6 7 8 9 10

zero one three four five six seven eight nine ten

three 3

0 1 2 4 5 6 7 8 9 10

zero one two four five six seven eight nine ten

four ⁘ 4

0 1 2 3 5 6 7 8 9 10

zero one two three five six seven eight nine ten

five 5

0 1 2 3 4 6 7 8 9 10

zero one two three four six seven eight nine ten

six ⚄ ⚀ 6

0 1 2 3 4 5 7 8 9 10

zero one two three four five seven eight nine ten

seven ⚄ ⚁

0 1 2 3 4 5 6 8 9 10

zero one two three four five six eight nine ten

eight 8

0 1 2 3 4 5 6 7 9 10

zero one two three four five six seven nine ten

nine ⚄⚃ 9

0 1 2 3 4 5 6 7 8 10

zero one two three four five six seven eight ten

ten ⚄ ⚄ 10

0 1 2 3 4 5 6 7 8 9

zero one two three four five six seven eight nine

‘Line up!’ bellows the captain.

Point to pirates one to ten.

'Someone's missing!'

Can you see who it is?

'Tidy up this mess!'

Can you match the pairs?

‘Who is working hardest?’

Who has the most fish?
Who has the least cannon balls?

'Help! It's an octopus!'

Who was first up the mast?
Who was fourth?

‘Teatime!’ shouts the cook.

How many blue fish are there?
How many red fish? How many altogether?

ten 10

0 1 2 3 4 5 6 7 8 9

zero one two three four five six seven eight nine

nine

0	1	2	3	4	5	6	7	8	10
zero	one	two	three	four	five	six	seven	eight	ten

eight 8

0 1 2 3 4 5 6 7 9 10

zero one two three four five six seven nine ten

seven ⚄ ⚁ 7

0 1 2 3 4 5 6 8 9 10

zero one two three four five six eight nine ten

six

0 1 2 3 4 5 7 8 9 10

zero one two three four five seven eight nine ten

five ⚄ 5

0 1 2 3 4 6 7 8 9 10

zero one two three four six seven eight nine ten

four ⁙

0	1	2	3	5	6	7	8	9	10
zero	one	two	three	five	six	seven	eight	nine	ten

three ⚂ 3

0 1 2 4 5 6 7 8 9 10

zero one two four five six seven eight nine ten

two

0	1		3	4	5	6	7	8	9	10
zero	one		three	four	five	six	seven	eight	nine	ten

one ⚀

0 2 3 4 5 6 7 8 9 10

zero two three four five six seven eight nine ten

zero

0	1	2	3	4	5	6	7	8	9	10
zero	one	two	three	four	five	six	seven	eight	nine	ten

Notes for parents and teachers

one parrot

six stripes

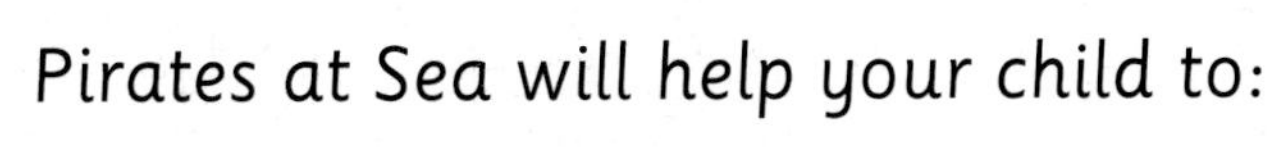
Pirates at Sea will help your child to:

- Recognize numbers.
- Count up from zero to ten, and down from ten to zero.
- Find one more and one less than any number from one to ten.
- Begin to add by putting two groups of things together.
- Spot pairs.

seven hooks

two pigtails

The story starts with zero – an empty sea. Then the pirates appear one by one. The pirates all have their own number. The third pirate has three buckles, the ninth pirate has nine spots on his jumper, and so on. Look out for the pirates in their place on the number line under each picture.

The next six pages each have a different number activity:

three buckles

eight coins

- Point to the pirates in order from one to ten.
- Spot the missing number.
- Find the matching pairs.
- Learn about 'most' and 'least'.

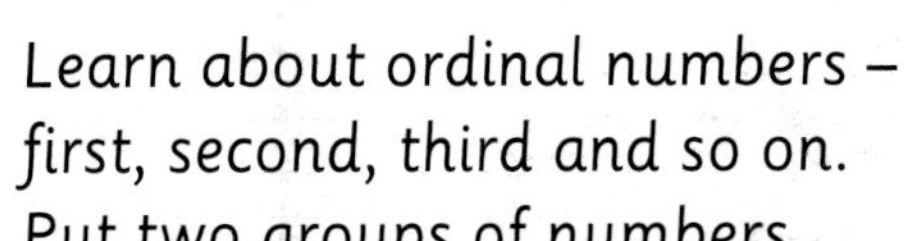

- Learn about ordinal numbers – first, second, third and so on.
- Put two groups of numbers together and begin to add.

After a hard day's work the pirates go to bed. Count them as they disappear one by one. The book ends where it began – with zero.

four bracelets

nine spots

Try these activities and games to help you learn about everyday numbers.

• The pirates line up in order, one to ten. Muddle up some plastic numbers or number cards. Can you arrange them in order?

• One of the pirates goes missing. Leave out a number as you count to ten. What is the missing number?

• One pirate has caught the most fish. Make piles of bricks, books or anything at all. Guess which pile has most and which has least. Count and see if you are right.

• When a giant octopus scares the pirates, the captain is first up the mast! Watch traffic going down the street – a blue car goes by first, a bus second, a lorry third and so on.

five weapons

ten buttons

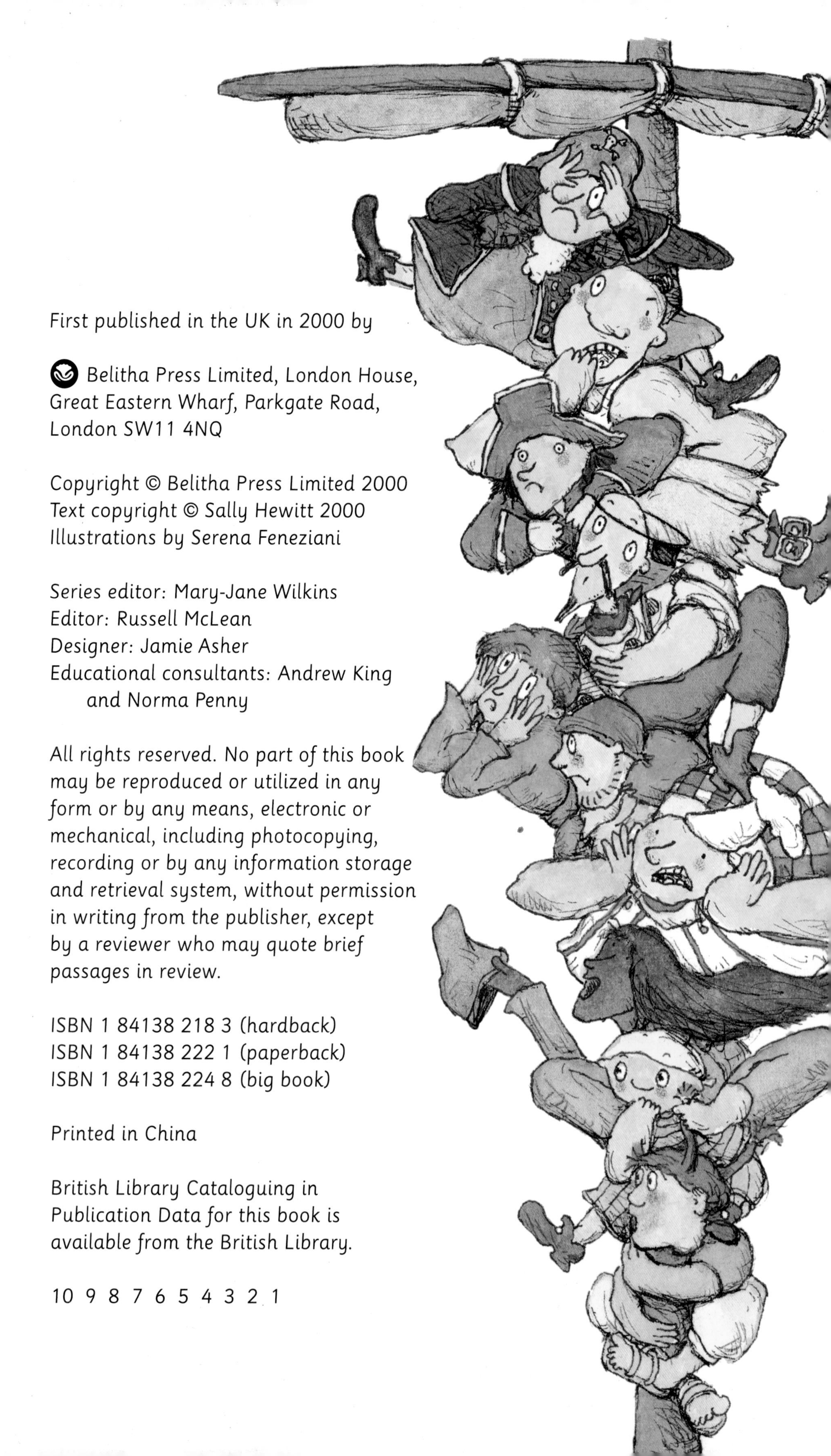

First published in the UK in 2000 by

Belitha Press Limited, London House,
Great Eastern Wharf, Parkgate Road,
London SW11 4NQ

Illustrations by Serena Feneziani

Series editor: Mary-Jane Wilkins
Editor: Russell McLean
Designer: Jamie Asher
Educational consultants: Andrew King
and Norma Penny

ISBN 1 84138 218 3 (hardback)
ISBN 1 84138 222 1 (paperback)
ISBN 1 84138 224 8 (big book)

Printed in China

British Library Cataloguing in Publication Data for this book is available from the British Library.

10 9 8 7 6 5 4 3 2 1